RIBS
AND MORE

Publications International, Ltd.

Pictured on the front cover: Bodacious Grilled Ribs *(page 22)*.

ISBN: 978-1-4508-9339-8

Library of Congress Control Number: 2014950496

Manufactured in China.

8 7 6 5 4 3 2 1

Microwave Cooking: Microwave ovens vary in wattage. Use
the cooking times as guidelines and check for doneness before
adding more time.

Preparation/Cooking Times: Preparation times are based on
the approximate amount of time required to assemble the recipe
before cooking, baking, chilling or serving. These times include
preparation steps such as measuring, chopping and mixing.
The fact that some preparations and cooking can be done
simultaneously is taken into account. Preparation of optional
ingredients and serving suggestions is not included.

TABLE OF CONTENTS

GREAT GRILLED RIBS

CLASSIC BABY BACK RIBS
MAKES ABOUT 4 SERVINGS

3   to 4 pounds pork baby back ribs, cut into
      3-rib portions (2 to 3 racks)
1   cup CATTLEMEN'S® Award Winning Classic
      Barbecue Sauce

1. Grill ribs over indirect heat on covered grill
for 1½ hours (or in a 350°F oven).

2. Baste with barbecue sauce. Cook 30 minutes
longer until meat is very tender. Serve with
additional barbecue sauce.

PREP TIME: 5 minutes
COOK TIME: 2 hours

TIP: To make Blazin' BBQ Wings, mix equal
amounts CATTLEMEN'S Award Winning
Classic Barbecue Sauce with FRANK'S®
RedHot® Original Cayenne Pepper Sauce
and coat cooked wings.

SPICY SMOKED BEEF RIBS

MAKES 4 TO 6 SERVINGS

- 4 wood pieces for smoking
- 4 to 6 pounds beef back ribs, cut into 3- to 4-rib portions
  Black pepper
- 1⅓ cups barbecue sauce
- 2 teaspoons hot pepper sauce or Szechuan chili sauce
  Beer, at room temperature, or hot water

1. Soak wood pieces in water at least 30 minutes; drain.

2. Spread ribs on large baking sheet; season with black pepper. Combine barbecue sauce and hot pepper sauce in small bowl. Brush ribs with half of sauce. Marinate in refrigerator 30 minutes to 1 hour.

3. Prepare grill for indirect cooking. Add soaked wood to fire. Place foil drip pan in center of grill. Fill pan half full with beer.

4. Place ribs on grid, meaty side up, directly above drip pan. Grill ribs, covered, over low heat about 1 hour or until tender, brushing remaining sauce over ribs 2 or 3 times during cooking. (If grill has thermometer, maintain cooking temperature at 250°F to 275°F.) Add additional soaked wood after 30 minutes, if necessary.

EASY GRILLED COUNTRY-STYLE RIBS

MAKES 6 SERVINGS

REYNOLDS WRAP® Heavy Duty Aluminum Foil

REYNOLDS WRAP® Non-Stick Aluminum Foil

Dry Seasoning Rub

- 2 tablespoons packed brown sugar
- 2 teaspoons *each* seasoned salt, grated lemon peel, garlic powder, onion powder, chili powder and paprika
- ¼ teaspoon black pepper
- ⅛ teaspoon cayenne pepper
- 3 pounds country-style pork ribs, cut in half
- 1¼ cups barbecue sauce, divided
- ¼ cup water

PREHEAT grill to medium-high or oven to 450°F.

COMBINE brown sugar, seasoned salt, lemon peel, garlic powder, onion powder, chili powder, paprika, black pepper and cayenne pepper in small bowl.

CENTER ribs in single layer on REYNOLDS WRAP® Heavy Duty Aluminum Foil. Sprinkle seasoning rub over ribs and rub into meat, turning to coat evenly. Combine ¼ cup barbecue sauce and water. Spoon over ribs, turning to coat evenly. Reserve remaining barbecue sauce for grilling ribs.

BRING up foil sides. Double fold top and ends to seal making one large foil packet, leaving room for heat circulation inside.

GRILL on covered grill **OR BAKE** 20 minutes. Remove foil packet. Place ribs on REYNOLDS WRAP® Non-Stick Aluminum Foil with non-stick (dull) side facing up.

Continue grilling or broil 15 minutes, brushing with reserved barbecue sauce, turning once.

APRICOT AND HONEY GLAZED BABY BACK RIBS

MAKES 6 TO 8 SERVINGS

- 1 tablespoon garlic powder
- 1 tablespoon ground cumin
- 1 teaspoon salt
- ½ teaspoon black pepper
- 6 pounds pork baby back ribs (2 racks), halved
- 1 bottle (12 ounces) honey wheat lager
- 1 cup apricot preserves
- 3 tablespoons honey

1. Prepare grill for indirect cooking. Oil grid.

2. Combine garlic powder, cumin, salt and pepper in small bowl; mix well. Rub over both sides of ribs.

3. Grill ribs, meaty side down, over medium heat 30 minutes. Turn and grill 30 minutes.

4. Meanwhile, combine lager, preserves and honey in medium saucepan; bring to a boil over medium-high heat. Cook 20 minutes or until thickened and reduced to ¾ cup.

5. Turn and brush ribs with half of glaze; grill 15 minutes. Turn and brush with remaining glaze; grill 15 minutes or until ribs are tender.

CAVEMEN BEEF BACK RIBS

MAKES 6 TO 8 SERVINGS

- ¼ cup paprika
- ¼ cup brown sugar
- ¼ cup seasoned salt
- 2 full racks beef back ribs, split in half (about 6 to 8 pounds)
- 1 cup CATTLEMEN'S® Authentic Smoke House Barbecue Sauce
- ¼ cup apple, pineapple or orange juice

1. Combine paprika, sugar and seasoned salt. Rub mixture into ribs. Cover ribs and refrigerate 1 to 3 hours.

2. Prepare grill for indirect cooking over medium-low heat (250°F). Place ribs on rib rack or in foil pan. Cook on covered grill 2½ to 3 hours until very tender.

3. Meanwhile, combine barbecue sauce and juice. Brush mixture on ribs during last 30 minutes of cooking. Serve with additional barbecue sauce.

PREP TIME: 5 minutes
COOK TIME: 3 hours
MARINATE TIME: 1 hour

TIP: For very tender ribs, remove membrane from underside of ribs before cooking. With a sharp paring knife, score membrane on bone from underside of ribs. Lift up portions of membrane with point of knife. Using kitchen towel, pull membrane away from bone and discard.

SEASONED BABY BACK RIBS

MAKES 6 SERVINGS

1   tablespoon paprika

1½ teaspoons garlic salt

1   teaspoon celery salt

½   teaspoon black pepper

¼   teaspoon ground red pepper

4   pounds pork baby back ribs, cut into
     3- to 4-rib portions, well trimmed

     Barbecue Sauce (recipe follows)

1. Preheat oven to 350°F. Line shallow roasting pan with foil.

2. Combine paprika, garlic salt, celery salt, black pepper and red pepper in small bowl. Rub over both sides of ribs. Place ribs in prepared pan; bake 30 minutes.

3. Meanwhile, prepare grill for direct cooking. Prepare Barbecue Sauce.

4. Grill ribs, covered, over medium heat 10 minutes.

5. Remove ribs from rib rack with tongs; brush half of Barbecue Sauce over both sides of ribs. Return ribs to rib rack. Grill, covered, 10 minutes or until ribs are tender and browned. Serve with reserved sauce.

BARBECUE SAUCE: Combine ½ cup ketchup, ⅓ cup packed brown sugar, 1 tablespoon cider vinegar, 2 teaspoons Worcestershire sauce and 2 teaspoons soy sauce in small bowl; mix well. Reserve half of sauce for serving.

KANSAS CITY-STYLE SPARERIBS

MAKES 4 SERVINGS

2 sheets (18×24 inches each) REYNOLDS WRAP® Heavy Duty Aluminum Foil

Dry Rub

¼ cup packed brown sugar

1 to 3 tablespoons salt

1 tablespoon chili powder

1 tablespoon black pepper

½ teaspoon ground allspice

½ teaspoon garlic powder

½ teaspoon onion powder

½ teaspoon celery salt

¼ teaspoon cayenne pepper

¼ teaspoon ground cumin

3 pounds pork spareribs, cut in half

½ cup water

¾ cup barbecue sauce

PREHEAT grill to medium. Combine ingredients for Dry Rub in small bowl; sprinkle over ribs and rub into meat, turning to coat evenly.

CENTER half of ribs in single layer on each sheet of REYNOLDS WRAP® Heavy Duty Aluminum Foil.

BRING up foil sides. Double fold top and one end. Through open end, add ½ cup water. Double fold remaining end to seal packet, leaving room for heat circulation inside. Repeat to make two packets.

GRILL 45 to 60 minutes on covered grill. Carefully remove ribs from foil; place on grill and brush with barbecue sauce. Continue grilling 10 to 15 minutes, brushing with sauce and turning every 5 minutes.

BLACK MAGIC RIBS

MAKES 4 SERVINGS

- 2 cups PACE® Picante Sauce
- 2 tablespoons Worcestershire sauce
- 2 tablespoons balsamic vinegar
- 2 tablespoons molasses
- 2 tablespoons ground coffee beans
- 2 tablespoons unsweetened cocoa powder
- 2 cloves garlic, minced
- 4 pounds pork spareribs
- 2 green onions, finely chopped (about ¼ cup)

1. Stir the picante sauce, Worcestershire, vinegar, molasses, coffee, cocoa powder and garlic in a medium bowl. Pour *half* the marinade into a 3-quart shallow baking dish. Add the ribs and turn to coat. Cover and refrigerate for 12 hours. Cover and refrigerate the remaining picante sauce mixture.

2. Lightly oil the grill rack. Heat the grill to medium with the grill set up for indirect cooking. Grill for 3 to 4 hours or until the ribs are fork-tender, turning and basting often with the marinade.

3. Heat the reserved picante sauce mixture in a 1-quart saucepan over medium heat to a boil. Serve the sauce with the ribs and garnish with the onions.

PREP TIME: 12 hours 15 minutes
COOK TIME: 3 hours
TOTAL TIME: 15 hours 15 minutes

SPICY HUNAN RIBS

MAKES 4 TO 6 SERVINGS

1⅓ cups hoisin sauce or CATTLEMEN'S® Golden Honey Barbecue Sauce

⅔ cup FRANK'S® REDHOT® XTRA Hot Cayenne Pepper Sauce or FRANK'S® REDHOT® Cayenne Pepper Sauce

¼ cup soy sauce

2 tablespoons brown sugar

2 tablespoons dark sesame oil

2 tablespoons grated peeled ginger root

4 cloves garlic, crushed through a press

2 full racks pork spareribs, trimmed (about 6 pounds)

1. Combine hoisin sauce, Frank's RedHot XTRA Hot Sauce, soy sauce, brown sugar, sesame oil, ginger and garlic; mix well.

2. Place ribs into large resealable plastic food storage bags. Pour 1½ cups sauce mixture over ribs. Seal bags and marinate in refrigerator 1 to 3 hours or overnight.

3. Prepare grill for indirect cooking over medium-low heat (250°F). Place ribs on rib rack or in foil pan; discard marinade. Cook on covered grill 2½ to 3 hours until very tender. Baste with remaining sauce during last 15 minutes of cooking. If desired, grill ribs over direct heat at end of cooking to char slightly.

PREP TIME: 5 minutes
MARINATE TIME: 1 hour
COOK TIME: 3 hours

TIP: Use Kansas City or St. Louis-style ribs for this recipe.

BODACIOUS GRILLED RIBS

MAKES 4 SERVINGS

2   tablespoons paprika

2   teaspoons dried basil

½   teaspoon onion powder

¼   teaspoon garlic powder

¼   teaspoon ground red pepper

¼   teaspoon black pepper

4   pounds pork loin back ribs

2   sheets (24×18 inches each) heavy-duty foil, lightly sprayed with nonstick cooking spray

8   ice cubes

1   cup barbecue sauce

½   cup apricot fruit spread

1. Prepare grill for direct cooking. Cut ribs into 4- to 6-rib portions.

2. Combine paprika, basil, onion powder, garlic powder, red pepper and black pepper in small bowl. Rub over both sides of ribs. Place 2 pounds of ribs in single layer in center of each foil sheet. Place 4 ice cubes on top of each layer of ribs.

3. Double-fold sides and ends of foil to seal packets, leaving head space for heat circulation.

4. Grill packets, covered, over medium heat 45 to 60 minutes or until ribs are tender. Carefully open one end of each packet to allow steam to escape.

5. Combine barbecue sauce and fruit spread in small bowl. Place ribs directly on grid; brush with barbecue sauce mixture. Grill 5 to 10 minutes, brushing with sauce and turning frequently.

ASIAN PEACH GLAZED RIBS

MAKES 5 TO 6 SERVINGS

2 sheets (18×24 inches each) REYNOLDS WRAP® Heavy Duty Aluminum Foil

3 pounds baby back pork ribs

½ cup water, divided

Seasoning Rub

1 tablespoon packed brown sugar

1 teaspoon 5-spice powder or ground ginger

1 teaspoon celery salt

½ teaspoon paprika

¼ teaspoon ground red pepper

Glaze

⅔ cup peach preserves

2 teaspoons lemon juice

1 teaspoon soy sauce

PREHEAT grill to medium. Cut each rack of ribs into thirds. Center half of ribs in single layer on each sheet of REYNOLDS WRAP® Heavy Duty Aluminum Foil.

COMBINE ingredients for Seasoning Rub. Sprinkle over ribs and rub into meat, turning to coat evenly.

BRING up foil sides. Double fold top and one end. Through open end, pour in ¼ cup water. Double fold remaining end to seal packet, leaving room for heat circulation inside. Repeat to make two packets.

GRILL 45 to 60 minutes on covered grill. Carefully remove ribs from foil; place directly on grill.

COMBINE peach preserves, lemon juice and soy sauce in small bowl. Brush ribs generously with Glaze. Continue grilling 10 to 15 minutes on uncovered grill, brushing with Glaze and turning every 5 minutes. Discard any remaining Glaze.

REYNOLDS KITCHENS TIP:

Three or four ice cubes may be substituted for the water in each packet of ribs, if desired.

JERK-STYLE BABY BACK RIBS

MAKES 4 SERVINGS

2 racks well-trimmed pork baby back ribs
   (about 3½ pounds)

2 tablespoons Caribbean jerk seasoning

½ cup hickory-flavored barbecue sauce

2 tablespoons Pickapeppa sauce*

½ teaspoon red pepper flakes

*Pickapeppa sauce is a tangy Jamaican sauce found in the supermarket's condiment aisle. If Pickapeppa is not available, substitute 1 tablespoon Worcestershire sauce and 1 tablespoon lime juice.

1. Preheat oven to 375°F.

2. Cut each rack of ribs in half crosswise. Rub jerk seasoning over both sides of ribs. Place in shallow roasting pan; bake 45 to 60 minutes or until cooked through.

3. Meanwhile, combine barbecue sauce, Pickapeppa sauce and red pepper flakes in small bowl; mix well. Prepare grill for direct cooking.

4. Grill ribs over medium heat 8 minutes per side. Brush half of sauce over ribs; grill 2 minutes. Turn and brush remaining sauce over ribs; grill 2 to 3 minutes or until ribs are glazed.

BABY BACK BARBECUE RIBS

MAKES 5 TO 6 SERVINGS

- 2 sheets (18×24 inches each) REYNOLDS WRAP® Heavy Duty Aluminum Foil
- 3 pounds baby back pork ribs
- 1 tablespoon packed brown sugar
- 1 tablespoon paprika
- 2 teaspoons garlic powder
- 1½ teaspoons black pepper
- ½ cup water or 6 to 8 ice cubes
- 1½ cups barbecue sauce

PREHEAT grill to medium.

CENTER half of ribs on each sheet of REYNOLDS WRAP® Heavy Duty Aluminum Foil. Combine brown sugar, paprika, garlic powder and pepper in small bowl. Sprinkle over ribs and rub into meat, turning to coat evenly.

BRING up foil sides. Double fold top and one end to seal packet. Through open end, add ¼ cup of water or 3 to 4 ice cubes. Double fold remaining end, leaving room for heat circulation inside. Repeat to make two packets.

GRILL for 45 to 60 minutes on covered grill. Carefully remove ribs from foil; place directly on grill.

BRUSH ribs with barbecue sauce. Continue grilling 10 to 15 minutes, brushing with sauce and turning every 5 minutes.

TANGY BARBECUED LAMB

MAKES 6 SERVINGS

¾   cup chili sauce

½   cup beer (not light beer)

½   cup honey

¼   cup reduced-sodium Worcestershire sauce

¼   cup finely chopped onion

2   cloves garlic, minced

½   teaspoon red pepper flakes

¼   teaspoon sea salt

5   pounds lamb ribs, well trimmed and cut into individual ribs

1. Combine chili sauce, beer, honey, Worcestershire sauce, onion, garlic, red pepper flakes and salt in small saucepan; bring to a boil over medium-high heat. Reduce heat to low; cover and simmer 10 minutes. Remove from heat; let cool.

2. Place lamb in large resealable food storage bag; add chili sauce mixture. Seal bag; turn to coat. Marinate in refrigerator at least 2 hours, turning occasionally.

3. Prepare grill for indirect cooking. Oil grid.

4. Remove lamb from marinade; reserve marinade. Arrange lamb on grid over drip pan. Grill, covered, over medium heat 45 minutes, turning and brushing with marinade every 15 minutes. Place remaining marinade in small saucepan and bring to a boil; boil 1 minute. Serve with lamb.

TIP: To set up gas grill for indirect cooking, preheat all burners on high. Turn one burner off; place food over "off" burner. Reset remaining burner(s) to medium. Close lid to cook.

BARBECUED RIBS

MAKES 4 TO 6 SERVINGS

1 cup ketchup

½ cup GRANDMA'S® Molasses

¼ cup cider vinegar

¼ cup Dijon mustard

2 tablespoons Worcestershire sauce

1 teaspoon garlic powder

1 teaspoon hickory flavor liquid smoke (optional)

¼ teaspoon ground red pepper

¼ teaspoon hot pepper sauce

4 to 6 pounds baby back ribs

Prepare grill for direct cooking. While coals are heating, combine all ingredients except ribs in large bowl; mix well. Place ribs on grid over medium-hot coals. Cook ribs 40 to 45 minutes or until they begin to brown, turning occasionally.

Once ribs begin to brown, begin basting them with sauce. Continue to cook and baste ribs with sauce an additional 1 to 1½ hours or until tender and cooked through.*

Do not baste during last 5 minutes of grilling; discard remaining sauce.

BOLD AND ZESTY BEEF BACK RIBS

MAKES 5 TO 6 SERVINGS

5   pounds beef back ribs, cut into
      3- or 4-rib portions

    Salt and black pepper

1   teaspoon vegetable oil

1   small onion, minced

2   cloves garlic, minced

1   cup ketchup

½   cup chili sauce

2   tablespoons lemon juice

1   tablespoon packed brown sugar

1   teaspoon hot pepper sauce

1. Place ribs in shallow pan; season with salt and black pepper. Refrigerate until ready to grill.

2. Prepare grill for indirect cooking.

3. Meanwhile, prepare barbecue sauce. Heat oil in large saucepan over medium heat. Add onion and garlic; cook and stir 5 minutes or until onion is tender. Stir in ketchup, chili sauce, lemon juice, brown sugar and hot pepper sauce. Reduce heat to medium-low; cook 15 minutes, stirring occasionally.

4. Place ribs on grid directly over drip pan. Baste ribs generously with sauce. Grill, covered, 45 to 60 minutes or until ribs are tender and browned, turning occasionally.

5. Bring remaining sauce to a boil over medium-high heat; boil 1 minute. Serve ribs with sauce.

BARBECUED PORK SPARERIBS

MAKES 4 SERVINGS

4   pounds pork spareribs, cut into serving-size pieces

1   can (10¼ ounces) CAMPBELL'S® Beef Gravy

¾   cup barbecue sauce

2   tablespoons packed brown sugar

1. Place the ribs into an 8-quart saucepot and add water to cover. Heat over medium-high heat to a boil. Reduce the heat to low. Cover and cook for 30 minutes or until the meat is tender. Drain the ribs well in a colander.

2. Stir the gravy, barbecue sauce and brown sugar in a large bowl. Add the ribs and toss to coat.

3. Lightly oil the grill rack and heat the grill to medium-high. Grill the ribs for 10 minutes, turning and brushing occasionally with the gravy mixture, until the ribs are well glazed.

PREP TIME: 15 minutes
COOK TIME: 35 minutes
GRILL TIME: 10 minutes

KITCHEN TIP: Use the gravy mixture as a basting sauce when grilling chicken.

KOREAN BEEF SHORT RIBS

MAKES 4 TO 6 SERVINGS

2½ pounds beef chuck flanken-style short ribs, cut ⅜ to ½ inch thick*

¼ cup chopped green onions

¼ cup water

¼ cup soy sauce

1 tablespoon sugar

2 teaspoons grated fresh ginger

2 teaspoons dark sesame oil

2 cloves garlic, minced

½ teaspoon black pepper

1 tablespoon sesame seeds, toasted

*Flanken-style ribs can be ordered from your butcher. They are cross-cut short ribs sawed through the bones.

1. Place ribs in large resealable food storage bag. Combine green onions, water, soy sauce, sugar, ginger, oil, garlic and pepper in small bowl; pour over ribs. Seal bag; turn to coat. Marinate in refrigerator at least 4 hours or up to 8 hours, turning occasionally.

2. Prepare grill for direct cooking. Remove ribs from marinade; reserve marinade.

3. Grill ribs, covered, over medium-high heat 5 minutes. Brush lightly with reserved marinade; turn and brush again. Discard remaining marinade. Grill, covered, 5 to 6 minutes until medium or to desired doneness. Sprinkle with sesame seeds.

KANSAS CITY-STYLE RIBS

MAKES 6 SERVINGS

- 2   sheets (18×24 inches each) REYNOLDS WRAP® Heavy Duty Aluminum Foil
- 3   pounds baby back pork ribs
- ½   cup water
- ½   teaspoon liquid smoke
- 2   tablespoons butter or vegetable oil
- ½   cup finely chopped onion
- 2   cups ketchup
- ¼   cup Worcestershire sauce
- ¼   cup cider vinegar
- 1   tablespoon prepared mustard
- 1   tablespoon molasses
- ½   teaspoon ground cumin

PREHEAT grill to medium. Cut each rack of ribs into thirds. Center half of ribs in single layer on each sheet of REYNOLDS WRAP® Heavy Duty Aluminum Foil.

BRING up foil sides. Double fold top and one end. Through open end, add ¼ cup water and ¼ teaspoon liquid smoke. Double fold remaining end to seal packet, leaving room for heat circulation inside. Repeat to make two packets.

GRILL 45 to 60 minutes on covered grill. Melt butter in medium saucepan over medium-high heat. Add onion and cook until tender. Add remaining ingredients. Simmer over medium-low heat 20 to 25 minutes. Carefully remove ribs from foil; place directly on grill.

BRUSH ribs generously with sauce. Continue grilling 10 to 15 minutes on medium on uncovered grill, brushing with sauce and turning every 5 minutes.

OVEN & STOVETOP RIBS

EASY SUCCULENT SAUCY SPARERIBS

MAKES 6 SERVINGS

- 1 cup Italian vinaigrette dressing
- 1 cup RAGU® OLD WORLD STYLE® Traditional Pasta Sauce
- ¼ cup finely chopped onion
- ¼ cup firmly packed brown sugar
- 5 pounds spareribs, cut into 3-rib portions

1. Preheat oven to 300°F.

2. Combine all ingredients except spareribs in small bowl. Arrange ribs in broiler pan without rack and top with sauce. Cover tightly with aluminum foil and bake 2½ hours or until ribs are tender.

3. Drain fat from sauce and thicken sauce, if desired. Serve with ribs.

PREP TIME: 10 minutes
COOK TIME: 2 hours 30 minutes

SLOW-ROASTED ASIAN SHORT RIBS

MAKES 4 SERVINGS

- ½ cup teriyaki sauce
- 1 tablespoon rice vinegar
- 2 cloves garlic, minced
- 1 teaspoon dark sesame oil
- ⅛ teaspoon red pepper flakes
- 3 to 3½ pounds beef short ribs, cut into 2-inch portions
  Sesame seeds (optional)

1. Combine teriyaki sauce, vinegar, garlic, sesame oil and red pepper flakes in small bowl; mix well. Place ribs in large baking dish; pour teriyaki mixture over ribs and turn to coat. Cover and marinate in refrigerator at least 4 hours or overnight.

2. Preheat oven to 300°F. Cover ribs with foil and bake about 3 hours or until tender, turning twice.

3. *Turn oven to broil.* Place ribs on foil-lined baking sheet; broil 5 inches from heat source about 5 minutes or until browned and crisp. Sprinkle with sesame seeds, if desired.

GINGER PLUM SPARERIBS

MAKES ABOUT 20 APPETIZER OR 4 MAIN-DISH SERVINGS

- 1 jar (10 ounces) damson plum preserves or apple jelly
- ⅓ cup KARO® Light or Dark Corn Syrup
- ⅓ cup soy sauce
- ¼ cup chopped green onions
- 2 cloves garlic, minced
- 2 teaspoons ground ginger
- 2 pounds pork spareribs, trimmed, cut into serving pieces

1. In small saucepan, combine preserves, corn syrup, soy sauce, green onions, garlic and ginger. Stirring constantly, cook over medium heat until melted and smooth.

2. Pour into 11×7×2-inch baking dish. Add ribs, turning to coat. Cover; refrigerate several hours or overnight, turning once.

3. Remove ribs from marinade; place on rack in shallow baking pan.

4. Bake in 350°F oven about 1 hour or until tender, turning occasionally and basting with marinade. Do not baste during last 5 minutes of cooking.

PREP TIME: 15 minutes, plus marinating
BAKE TIME: 1 hour

SPICY PORK PO' BOYS

MAKES 4 SERVINGS

- 2 tablespoons chili powder
- 1 tablespoon salt
- 1 tablespoon onion powder
- 1 tablespoon granulated garlic
- 1 tablespoon paprika
- 1 tablespoon black pepper
- 1 teaspoon ground red pepper
- 1 pound boneless pork ribs
- ½ cup cola
- 1 tablespoon hot pepper sauce
- Dash Worcestershire sauce
- ½ cup ketchup
- 4 French rolls, toasted
- ½ cup prepared coleslaw

1. Combine chili powder, salt, onion powder, garlic, paprika, black pepper and red pepper in small bowl. Rub mixture over pork, coating all sides. Cover and refrigerate at least 3 hours or overnight.

2. Preheat oven to 250°F. Place ribs in Dutch oven. Combine cola, hot pepper sauce and Worcestershire sauce in small bowl; drizzle over ribs.

3. Cover and bake about 4 hours or until ribs are fork-tender. Remove ribs to large bowl.

4. Stir ketchup into Dutch oven; cook 4 to 6 minutes or until sauce has thickened, stirring frequently. Pour sauce over ribs, pulling meat apart with two forks and coating meat with sauce. Serve on rolls with coleslaw.

BBQ SHORT RIBS

MAKES 8 SERVINGS

4½   pounds beef short ribs, cut into individual
      rib pieces

1   can (10¾ ounces) CAMPBELL'S® Condensed
     Tomato Soup

2   tablespoons cider vinegar

2   tablespoons molasses

1   tablespoon Worcestershire sauce

1   clove garlic, minced

¼   teaspoon dried thyme leaves, crushed

1   large sweet onion, diced (about 1 cup)

1. Season the ribs as desired. Heat a 6-quart oven-safe saucepot oven medium-high heat. Add the ribs and cook until they're browned on all sides, about 15 minutes. Remove the ribs from the saucepot. Pour off any fat.

2. Add the soup, vinegar, molasses, Worcestershire, garlic, thyme and onion. Heat to a boil. Return the ribs to the saucepot. Cover the saucepot.

3. Bake at 350°F. for 1 hour or until the ribs are fork-tender.

PREP TIME: 15 minutes
COOK TIME: 1 hour 20 minutes
TOTAL TIME: 1 hour 35 minutes

HONEY-GLAZED SPARERIBS

MAKES ABOUT 4 SERVINGS

1 rack pork spareribs* (about 2 pounds)

¼ cup plus 1 tablespoon soy sauce, divided

3 tablespoons hoisin sauce

3 tablespoons dry sherry, divided

1 tablespoon sugar

2 cloves garlic, minced

1 teaspoon minced fresh ginger

¼ teaspoon Chinese five-spice powder

2 tablespoons honey

1 tablespoon cider vinegar

Sesame seeds (optional)

Ask your butcher to cut ribs down length of rack into two pieces so that each half is 2 to 3 inches wide.

1. Cut between bones of ribs to make 6-inch pieces. Trim excess fat. Place ribs in large resealable food storage bag.

2. Combine ¼ cup soy sauce, hoisin sauce, 2 tablespoons sherry, sugar, garlic, ginger and five-spice powder in small bowl; pour over ribs. Seal bag; turn to coat. Marinate in refrigerator 8 hours or overnight, turning bag occasionally.

3. Preheat oven to 350°F. Line large baking pan with foil. Place ribs on rack in pan, reserving marinade.

4. Bake 30 minutes. Turn ribs; brush with marinade. Bake 40 minutes or until ribs are tender.

5. Combine honey, vinegar, remaining 1 tablespoon soy sauce and 1 tablespoon sherry in small bowl; mix well. Brush half of mixture over ribs. *Turn oven to broil;* broil 4 to 6 inches from heat source 2 to 3 minutes or until glazed. Turn ribs and brush with remaining honey mixture; broil until glazed. Cut into serving-size pieces; sprinkle with sesame seeds, if desired.

ENCHILADA SLOW-ROASTED BABY BACK RIBS

MAKES 6 TO 8 SERVINGS

- 1 packet (1.25 ounces) ORTEGA® Reduced Sodium Fajita Seasoning Mix
- ¼ cup packed brown sugar
- 4 slabs baby back ribs (about 10 pounds)
- ½ cup Dijon mustard
- 2 jars (8 ounces each) ORTEGA® Enchilada Sauce

PREHEAT oven to 250°F. Combine seasoning mix and brown sugar in small bowl. Place large piece of aluminum foil on counter. On foil, brush both sides of ribs with mustard; sprinkle both sides with seasoning mixture.

ADJUST one oven rack to low position. Place foil-lined baking sheet on lower rack to collect drippings from ribs. Remove remaining oven rack; arrange ribs on rack. Slide rack with ribs into upper-middle position in oven.

ROAST ribs 1½ to 2 hours or until tender. Remove ribs from oven. Turn on broiler.

BRUSH enchilada sauce onto both sides of ribs. Transfer ribs to foil-lined baking sheet, meat side down. Broil 5 to 6 minutes or until sauce begins to bubble. Let stand 5 minutes before slicing into individual servings.

PREP TIME: 15 minutes
START TO FINISH TIME: 2 hours

TIP: You can also grill the ribs. Follow the same procedures, keeping the grill temperature at about 250°F and grill with the cover on until tender.

LITTLE RIBS IN PAPRIKA SAUCE

MAKES 6 TO 8 SERVINGS

1   rack pork baby back ribs (about 1½ pounds), cut into individual ribs

1   can (about 14 ounces) chicken broth

1   cup dry white wine or beer

1   tablespoon olive oil

2   teaspoons dried oregano

2   teaspoons smoked paprika or paprika

4   cloves garlic, minced

½   teaspoon salt

¼   teaspoon black pepper

1. Combine ribs, broth, wine, oil, oregano, paprika, garlic, salt and pepper in large saucepan; bring to a boil over medium-high heat. Reduce heat to low; cover and simmer 1 hour or until meat is tender and begins to separate from bones.

2. Remove ribs to serving plate; keep warm. Skim and discard fat from cooking liquid. Bring to a boil over medium heat. Reduce heat to low; simmer until sauce is reduced by half. Spoon sauce over ribs.

BRAISED SHORT RIBS WITH GRAVY

MAKES 6 SERVINGS

3½ pounds beef short ribs, trimmed of fat

½ cup all-purpose flour

2 tablespoons olive oil

2 large onions, chopped

2 cloves garlic, finely chopped

2 tablespoons tomato paste

2 tubs KNORR® Homestyle Stock–Beef

5 cups water

4 large carrots, cut into chunks

1. Preheat oven to 350°F. Season ribs, if desired, with salt and black pepper. Toss ribs with flour in plastic bag to lightly coat, shaking off excess; set aside.

2. Heat oil in 6-quart Dutch oven or ovenproof heavy-duty saucepan over medium-high heat and thoroughly brown short ribs on all sides. Remove short ribs and keep warm. Reserve 2 tablespoons drippings in Dutch oven.

3. Add onions and garlic to reserved drippings and cook, stirring frequently, until tender and golden, about 5 minutes. Stir in tomato paste and cook, stirring frequently, until well browned. Stir in KNORR® Homestyle Stock–Beef and water.

4. Return short ribs to Dutch oven and bring to a boil over high heat; stir. Bake, covered, 1½ hours. Add carrots and continue baking an additional 30 minutes until ribs and carrots are tender.

5. Remove ribs to serving dish and keep warm; skim fat from gravy. Bring gravy to a boil and continue boiling over medium heat until slightly thickened, about 5 minutes. Pour gravy over ribs to serve.

MAPLE-MUSTARD PORTER RIBS

MAKES ABOUT 8 APPETIZER SERVINGS

1   cup porter

½   cup maple syrup

3   tablespoons Worcestershire sauce

2   tablespoons spicy brown mustard

1   teaspoon salt

¼   teaspoon black pepper

    Pinch ground red pepper

2   pounds pork baby back ribs, membrane removed from underside and cut in half

1. Combine porter, maple syrup, Worcestershire sauce, mustard, salt, black pepper and red pepper in medium saucepan; bring to a boil over medium-high heat. Reduce heat to low; simmer until reduced to ¾ cup, stirring occasionally. Pour into large bowl; cool to room temperature.

2. Set oven rack to middle position and preheat oven to 350°F. Line rimmed large baking sheet with two layers of foil and spray with nonstick cooking spray.

3. Place ribs in sauce, turning to coat. Arrange ribs, meaty side down, in single layer on prepared baking sheet; brush with remaining sauce. Cover tightly with foil.

4. Bake 50 minutes or until ribs are tender. Remove foil; turn ribs meaty side up. Brush ribs with liquid from baking sheet. *Turn oven to broil* (do not move oven rack or ribs); broil until ribs are glazed, brushing with remaining liquid from baking sheet every 3 minutes. Cool on baking sheet 10 minutes; remove to cutting board and cut into individual ribs.

BISTRO-STYLE SHORT RIBS

MAKES 4 SERVINGS

Vegetable cooking spray

3 pounds beef short ribs, cut into individual rib pieces

1 large onion, chopped (about 1 cup)

2 medium carrots, chopped (about ⅔ cup)

1 stalk celery, chopped (about ½ cup)

2¾ cups PREGO® Traditional *or* Marinara Italian Sauce

1¾ cups SWANSON® Beef Stock

1. Spray a 6-quart oven-safe saucepot with the cooking spray and heat over medium-high heat for 1 minute. Add the ribs in 2 batches and cook until they're browned on all sides. Remove the ribs from the saucepot. Pour off all but *2 tablespoons* fat.

2. Add the onion, carrots and celery to the saucepot and cook until they're tender. Stir the Italian sauce and stock in the saucepot and heat to a boil. Return the ribs to the saucepot. Cover the saucepot.

3. Bake at 350°F. for 1 hour 30 minutes or until the ribs are fork-tender.

PREP TIME: 10 minutes
COOK TIME: 1 hour 45 minutes
TOTAL TIME: 1 hour 55 minutes

FOR SLOW-COOKED BISTRO-STYLE RIBS: Brown the ribs in a 12-inch skillet as directed in step 1. Place the onion, carrots and celery in a 5-quart slow cooker. Top with the ribs. Pour the Italian sauce and stock in the cooker. Cover and cook on LOW for 7 to 8 hours or on HIGH for 3½ to 4 hours or until the ribs are fork-tender.

BARBECUED RIBS

MAKES 4 MAIN-DISH OR 8 APPETIZER SERVINGS

- 3 to 4 pounds lean pork baby back ribs or spareribs
- ⅓ cup hoisin sauce
- 4 tablespoons soy sauce, divided
- 3 tablespoons dry sherry
- 3 cloves garlic, minced
- 2 tablespoons honey
- 1 tablespoon dark sesame oil

1. Place ribs in large resealable food storage bag. Combine hoisin sauce, 3 tablespoons soy sauce, sherry and garlic in small bowl; pour over ribs. Seal bag; turn to coat. Marinate in refrigerator at least 4 hours or up to 24 hours.

2. Preheat oven to 375°F. Line shallow roasting pan with foil. Drain ribs; reserve marinade. Place ribs on rack in prepared pan.

3. Bake 30 minutes; turn and brush ribs with half of reserved marinade. Bake 15 minutes; turn and brush ribs with remaining marinade. Bake 15 minutes.

4. Combine remaining 1 tablespoon soy sauce, honey and sesame oil in small bowl; brush over ribs. Bake 5 to 10 minutes or until ribs are cooked through, browned and crisp.* Cut into serving pieces.

Ribs may be made ahead to this point. Cover and refrigerate up to 3 days. To reheat, wrap ribs in foil; cook in preheated 350°F oven 40 minutes or until heated through.

OVEN & STOVETOP RIBS 65

SWEET GINGERED SPARERIBS

MAKES 4 TO 6 SERVINGS

½ cup reduced-sodium soy sauce

⅓ cup honey

¼ cup dry sherry

1 clove garlic, minced

½ teaspoon ground ginger

4 pounds pork spareribs, cut into individual ribs or 2-rib portions

1. Preheat oven to 350°F. Combine soy sauce, honey, sherry, garlic and ginger in small bowl; mix well. Line rimmed baking sheet with foil.

2. Arrange ribs on prepared baking sheet, meaty side down. Brush soy sauce mixture generously over ribs. Cover loosely with foil.

3. Bake 1 hour. Remove foil. Turn ribs; brush generously with additional soy sauce mixture. Bake, uncovered, 30 minutes or until ribs are tender, brushing occasionally with remaining soy sauce mixture.

LEMON-ORANGE
GLAZED RIBS
MAKES 4 SERVINGS

2 racks pork baby back ribs (about 3 pounds), cut into halves

2 tablespoons soy sauce

2 tablespoons orange juice

2 tablespoons lemon juice

2 cloves garlic, minced

¼ cup orange marmalade

1 tablespoon hoisin sauce

1. Place ribs in large resealable food storage bag. Combine soy sauce, orange juice, lemon juice and garlic in small bowl; pour over ribs. Seal bag; turn to coat. Marinate in refrigerator at least 4 hours or up to 24 hours, turning once.

2. Preheat oven to 350°F. Line shallow roasting pan with foil. Drain ribs; reserve marinade. Place ribs on rack in prepared pan. Brush half of marinade over ribs.

3. Bake 20 minutes; turn ribs and brush with remaining marinade. Bake 20 minutes. Remove ribs from oven; pour off drippings.

4. Whisk marmalade and hoisin sauce in small bowl until well blended; brush half of mixture over ribs. Bake 10 minutes; turn and brush with remaining marmalade mixture. Bake 10 minutes or until ribs are tender and browned.

SMOKIN' BABY BACK RIBS

MAKES 8 SERVINGS

- 4 pounds baby back pork spareribs
- 1 tablespoon olive oil
- 1 large sweet onion, chopped (about 1 cup)
- 1 can (10¾ ounces) CAMPBELL'S® Condensed Tomato Soup (Regular or Healthy Request®)
- ¼ cup packed brown sugar
- 2 tablespoons cider vinegar
- 2 to 4 teaspoons hot pepper sauce

1. Heat the oven to 400°F. Line a large roasting pan with aluminum foil. Place the ribs into the pan. Cover the pan.

2. Bake for 45 minutes. Uncover the pan and pour off any fat.

3. Heat the oil in a 2-quart saucepan over medium heat. Add the onion and cook until it's tender. Stir in the soup, brown sugar, vinegar and hot pepper sauce and heat to a boil. Reduce the heat to low. Cook for 5 minutes or until the sauce is slightly thickened.

4. Pour the soup mixture over the ribs.

5. Bake, uncovered, for 30 minutes or until the ribs are fork-tender. Cut the ribs into serving-sized pieces. Return the ribs to the pan and toss to coat with the sauce.

PREP TIME: 10 minutes
COOK TIME: 1 hour 15 minutes
TOTAL TIME: 1 hour 25 minutes

KITCHEN TIP: Prepare the sauce mixture while the ribs are baking.

BBQ SHORT RIBS WITH COLA SAUCE

MAKES 4 TO 6 SERVINGS

- 1 large (17×15 inches) foil bag
- 1 can (12 ounces) regular cola
- ¾ cup honey
- 1 can (6 ounces) tomato paste
- ½ cup cider vinegar
- 1 teaspoon salt
- 2 cloves garlic, minced
  Dash hot pepper sauce (optional)
- 4 pounds beef short ribs, cut into 2-inch pieces

1. Preheat oven to 450°F. Place foil bag on rimmed baking sheet. Spray inside of bag with nonstick cooking spray; dust with flour.

2. Combine cola, honey, tomato paste, vinegar, salt, garlic and hot pepper sauce, if desired, in medium saucepan; bring to a boil over medium-high heat. Reduce heat to medium; cook about 15 minutes, stirring occasionally, until slightly reduced.

3. Dip each short rib in sauce. Place ribs in single layer in prepared foil bag. Pour additional 1 cup sauce into bag. Seal bag, leaving headspace for heat circulation by folding open end twice.

4. Bake 1 hour 15 minutes or until ribs are cooked through. Carefully cut open bag.

SLOW COOKER SENSATIONS

HONEY BARBECUE RIBS

MAKES 4 SERVINGS

1 can (about 14 ounces) beef broth

½ cup water

3 tablespoons soy sauce

2 tablespoons honey

2 tablespoons maple syrup

2 tablespoons barbecue sauce

½ teaspoon dry mustard

2 pounds pork baby back ribs, trimmed and cut into 3- to 4-rib portions

1. Combine broth, water, soy sauce, honey, syrup, barbecue sauce and mustard in slow cooker; mix well. Add ribs.

2. Cover; cook on LOW 6 to 8 hours or on HIGH 4 to 6 hours or until ribs are tender. Serve with sauce.

ASIAN GLAZED SHORT RIBS

MAKES 4 SERVINGS

- 4 pounds beef short ribs
- 1 envelope LIPTON® RECIPE SECRETS® Onion Soup Mix
- ½ cup apricot preserves
- ½ cup chili sauce
- ¼ cup firmly packed brown sugar
- ¼ cup soy sauce
- 2 tablespoons apple cider vinegar
- 1 tablespoon cornstarch
- 1 cup water

1. In slow cooker, combine all ingredients except cornstarch and water.

2. Cook covered on LOW 8 to 10 hours or on HIGH 4 to 6 hours, or until ribs are tender.

3. Remove ribs to serving platter; keep warm. In small bowl, combine cornstarch with water. Stir into sauce and cook, covered, on HIGH 10 to 15 minutes or until thickened. Pour sauce over ribs.

PREP TIME: 4 minutes
COOK TIME: HIGH 4 hours, 10 minutes

COUNTRY-STYLE RIBS

MAKES 4 TO 6 SERVINGS

1 tablespoon vegetable oil

4 to 6 bone-in country-style pork ribs (2 to 3 pounds), trimmed of fat

Salt and black pepper

1½ cups chopped onion

1 bottle (20 to 24 ounces) ketchup

2 cups plus 2 tablespoons water, divided

1 jar (about 16 ounces) unsweetened applesauce

2 tablespoons packed brown sugar

½ teaspoon hot pepper sauce (optional)

1 tablespoon cornstarch

1. Heat oil in large skillet over medium-high heat. Season ribs with salt and pepper. Cook ribs in batches, turning to brown all sides. Remove to large plate.

2. Add onion to skillet; cook and stir until softened. Remove skillet from heat.

3. Combine ketchup, 2 cups water, applesauce, brown sugar and hot pepper sauce, if desired, in slow cooker; mix well. Stir in cooked onions and pan drippings. Add ribs, cutting to fit into slow cooker as necessary.

4. Cover; cook on LOW 6 to 8 hours or until ribs are very tender.

5. Remove ribs to large plate. Skim fat from sauce in slow cooker. Stir cornstarch into remaining 2 tablespoons water in small bowl until well blended. *Turn slow cooker to HIGH.* Stir mixture into sauce in slow cooker; cook on HIGH 5 to 10 minutes or until sauce begins to thicken.

6. Return ribs to thickened sauce; stir to coat.

MELT-IN-YOUR-MOUTH SHORT RIBS

MAKES 6 SERVINGS

6 serving-sized pieces beef short ribs (about 3 pounds)

2 tablespoons packed brown sugar

3 cloves garlic, minced

1 teaspoon dried thyme leaves, crushed

¼ cup all-purpose flour

1 can (10½ ounces) CAMPBELL'S® Condensed French Onion Soup

1 bottle (12 fluid ounces) dark ale or beer

Hot mashed potatoes or egg noodles

1. Place the beef into a 5-quart slow cooker. Add the brown sugar, garlic, thyme and flour and toss to coat.

2. Stir the soup and ale in a small bowl. Pour over the beef.

3. Cover and cook on LOW for 8 to 9 hours* or until the beef is fork-tender. Serve with the mashed potatoes.

Or on HIGH for 4 to 5 hours.

PREP TIME: 10 minutes
COOK TIME: 8 hours
TOTAL TIME: 8 hours 10 minutes

SOUTH PACIFIC PORK RIBS

MAKES 4 TO 6 SERVINGS

1   to 2 tablespoons canola oil, divided

3½ to 4 pounds pork loin riblets (about 20 riblets)
     Salt and black pepper

1   onion, chopped

1   can (20 ounces) pineapple chunks in
     100% pineapple juice

¼   cup all-purpose flour

½   cup water

¼   cup vinegar

¼   cup packed brown sugar

¼   cup ketchup

1   tablespoon soy sauce

1. Heat 1 tablespoon oil in large skillet over medium-high heat. Season riblets with salt and pepper. Cook riblets in batches, turning to brown all sides and adding additional oil as needed. Place in slow cooker.

2. Add onion to skillet; cook and stir 3 to 5 minutes or until softened. Drain pineapple, reserving 1 cup juice. Whisk pineapple juice and flour in small bowl until well blended.

3. Add water, vinegar, brown sugar, ketchup and soy sauce to skillet; cook and stir until blended. Add juice mixture; cook and stir over medium-low heat until thickened. Stir in pineapple chunks. Pour sauce over ribs in slow cooker.

4. Cover; cook on LOW 8 to 10 hours or on HIGH 5 to 6 hours or until ribs are tender.

ITALIAN SHORT RIBS WITH MUSHROOMS

MAKES 4 TO 6 SERVINGS

3   pounds beef short ribs, trimmed of excess fat
    Salt and black pepper
1   to 2 tablespoons vegetable oil
2   large onions, sliced
2   packages (8 ounces each) baby bella or
    cremini mushrooms, cleaned and quartered
2   cups red wine
2   cups beef broth
2   cloves garlic, minced
2   teaspoons Italian seasoning

1. Spray slow cooker with nonstick cooking spray. Season ribs with salt and pepper. Heat 1 tablespoon oil in large skillet over medium-high heat. Cook ribs in batches, turning to brown all sides and adding additional oil as needed. Place in slow cooker.

2. Add onions to skillet; cook and stir 5 minutes or until translucent. Add mushrooms, wine, broth, garlic and Italian seasoning; bring to a simmer and cook 3 minutes. Pour over short ribs in slow cooker.

3. Cover; cook on LOW 10 to 12 hours or on HIGH 6 to 8 hours or until ribs are tender. Season to taste with salt and pepper. Remove ribs and mushrooms to serving plate. Strain cooking liquid; serve with ribs.

BRAISED SHORT RIBS WITH RED WINE TOMATO SAUCE

MAKES 8 SERVINGS

- 4 pounds beef short ribs, cut into serving-sized pieces
- 2⅔ cups PREGO® Fresh Mushroom Italian Sauce
- 1 cup dry red wine
- 1 bag fresh *or* frozen whole baby carrots
- 1 large onion, chopped (about 1 cup)
  Hot cooked rice

1. Season the ribs as desired.

2. Stir the Italian sauce, wine, carrots and onion in a 3½-quart slow cooker. Add the ribs and turn to coat.

3. Cover and cook on LOW for 7 to 8 hours* or until the ribs are fork-tender. Serve with the rice.

Or on HIGH for 4 to 5 hours.

PREP TIME: 10 minutes
COOK TIME: 7 hours
TOTAL TIME: 7 hours 10 minutes

SWEET AND SAUCY RIBS

MAKES 4 SERVINGS

2 pounds pork baby back ribs

1 teaspoon black pepper

2½ cups barbecue sauce (not mesquite flavored)

1 jar (8 ounces) cherry jam or preserves

1 tablespoon Dijon mustard

¼ teaspoon salt

1. Trim excess fat from ribs. Rub 1 teaspoon pepper over both sides of ribs. Cut ribs into 2-rib portions; place in slow cooker.

2. Combine barbecue sauce, jam, mustard and ¼ teaspoon salt in small bowl; pour over ribs.

3. Cover; cook on LOW 6 to 8 hours or until ribs are tender. Season with additional salt and pepper, if desired. Serve ribs with sauce.

CHINESE-STYLE SHORT RIBS

MAKES 4 TO 6 SERVINGS

- ½ cup beef broth
- ¼ cup dry sherry
- ¼ cup soy sauce
- 1 tablespoon honey
- 1 tablespoon grated fresh ginger
- 2 teaspoons minced garlic
- 3 pounds boneless beef short ribs
- 1 teaspoon salt
- ½ teaspoon black pepper
- ½ cup chopped green onions

Hot cooked rice (optional)

1. Combine broth, sherry, soy sauce, honey, ginger and garlic in slow cooker.

2. Season ribs with salt and pepper. Add to slow cooker, turning to coat both sides with sauce.

3. Cover; cook on LOW 7 to 8 hours or until ribs are fork-tender. Remove ribs to serving dish; sprinkle with green onions. Serve with rice, if desired.

TIP: To mince ginger quickly, peel a small piece and put it through a garlic press. Store the remaining unpeeled ginger in a small resealable food storage bag in the refrigerator for up to 3 weeks.

CAJUN-STYLE COUNTRY RIBS

MAKES 6 TO 8 SERVINGS

2 cups baby carrots

1 onion, coarsely chopped

1 green bell pepper, cut into 1-inch pieces

1 red bell pepper, cut into 1-inch pieces

2 teaspoons minced garlic

2 tablespoons Cajun or Creole seasoning, divided

3½ to 4 pounds country-style pork spareribs

1 can (about 14 ounces) stewed tomatoes, undrained

2 tablespoons water

1 tablespoon cornstarch

Hot cooked rice

1. Combine carrots, onion, bell peppers, garlic and 2 teaspoons Cajun seasoning in slow cooker; mix well.

2. Trim excess fat from ribs; cut into individual ribs. Sprinkle with 1 tablespoon Cajun seasoning; place in slow cooker. Pour tomatoes over ribs.

3. Cover; cook on LOW 6 to 8 hours.

4. Remove ribs and vegetables from slow cooker with slotted spoon. Let liquid stand 15 minutes; skim off fat.

5. *Turn slow cooker to HIGH.* Stir water into cornstarch and remaining 1 teaspoon Cajun seasoning in small bowl until smooth. Add to slow cooker; mix well. Cook, uncovered, on HIGH 15 minutes or until thickened. Return ribs and vegetables to sauce; stir gently to coat. Serve with rice.

ASIAN PORK RIBS WITH SPICY NOODLES

MAKES 4 SERVINGS

1 can (about 14 ounces) beef broth

½ cup water

¼ cup rice wine vinegar

1 tablespoon grated fresh ginger

1 cup dried sliced shiitake mushrooms (about 1 ounce)

¼ teaspoon red pepper flakes

1 tablespoon Chinese five-spice powder

1 tablespoon dark sesame oil

1 teaspoon ground ginger

1 teaspoon chili powder

2 racks pork baby back ribs (about 4 pounds)

¾ cup hoisin sauce, divided

1 pound thin rice noodles or spaghetti, cooked and drained

¼ cup thinly sliced green onions

¼ cup chopped fresh cilantro

1. Combine broth, water, vinegar, fresh ginger, mushrooms and red pepper flakes in slow cooker.

2. Combine five-spice powder, sesame oil, ground ginger and chili powder in small bowl; mix well. Cut rib racks in half; dry with paper towels. Rub spice mixture over both sides of ribs; brush with half of hoisin sauce. Add ribs to slow cooker (do not stir).

3. Cover; cook on LOW 8 to 10 hours or on HIGH 5 to 6 hours or until ribs are fork-tender. Remove ribs to plate; brush with remaining hoisin sauce. Skim off any fat from cooking liquid.

4. Place noodles in bowls. Ladle some of cooking liquid over noodles; sprinkle with green onions and cilantro. Slice ribs; serve over noodles.

SLOW COOKER ONIONY BRAISED SHORT RIBS

MAKES 4 SERVINGS

- 3 pounds beef short ribs
- 2½ cups water
- 1 envelope LIPTON® RECIPE SECRETS® Onion Soup Mix
- ¼ cup ketchup
- 2 tablespoons firmly packed brown sugar
- 2 tablespoons sherry (optional)
- ½ teaspoon ground ginger
- ¼ cup water
- 1 tablespoon all-purpose flour
- ¼ teaspoon ground black pepper

1. In slow cooker, arrange short ribs. Combine 2½ cups water with LIPTON® Recipe Secrets® Onion Soup Mix, ketchup, brown sugar, sherry, if desired, and ginger; pour over ribs.

2. Cook covered on LOW 8 to 10 hours or on HIGH 4 to 6 hours.

3. Remove ribs to serving platter; keep warm. In small bowl, combine ¼ cup water with flour and black pepper and stir into juices in slow cooker. Cook covered on HIGH 15 minutes or until thickened. Pour sauce over ribs.

PREP TIME: 10 minutes
COOK TIME: HIGH 4 hours, 15 minutes

BEST EVER BARBECUED RIBS

MAKES 6 SERVINGS

1 teaspoon salt

1 teaspoon dried thyme

1 teaspoon paprika

¼ teaspoon black pepper

⅛ teaspoon ground red pepper

3 to 3½ pounds well-trimmed pork baby back ribs, cut into 4-rib portions

¼ cup ketchup

2 tablespoons packed brown sugar

1 tablespoon Worcestershire sauce

1 tablespoon soy sauce

1. Spray slow cooker with nonstick cooking spray. Combine salt, thyme, paprika, black pepper and red pepper in small bowl; rub onto meaty side of ribs. Place ribs in slow cooker.

2. Cover; cook on LOW 7 to 8 hours or on HIGH 3 to 4 hours. Remove ribs to plate; discard liquid.

3. Combine ketchup, brown sugar, Worcestershire sauce and soy sauce in small bowl; mix well.

4. *Turn slow cooker to HIGH.* Coat ribs with sauce mixture; return to slow cooker. Cover; cook on HIGH 30 minutes or until ribs are glazed.

ASIAN GLAZED SHORT RIBS

MAKES 8 SERVINGS

- 1½ cups SWANSON® Beef Broth (Regular, 50% Less Sodium *or* Certified Organic)
- 1½ cups orange marmalade
- ⅓ cup chili sauce
- 2 tablespoons soy sauce
- 1 medium onion, thinly sliced (about ½ cup)
- 4 to 5 pounds beef short ribs

  Hot cooked jasmine *or* basmati rice

1. Stir the broth, marmalade, chili sauce, soy sauce and onion in a 6-quart slow cooker. Add the beef and turn to coat.

2. Cover and cook on LOW for 6 to 7 hours or until the beef is fork-tender. Serve with the rice.

PREP TIME: 10 minutes
COOK TIME: 6 to 7 hours

BACON AND STOUT BRAISED SHORT RIBS

MAKES 4 TO 6 SERVINGS

- 4 pounds beef short ribs, well trimmed
  Salt and black pepper
- 1 tablespoon vegetable oil
- 6 ounces thick-cut bacon, chopped
- 1 large onion, halved and sliced
- 2 tablespoons all-purpose flour
- 2 tablespoons spicy brown mustard
- 1 tablespoon tomato paste
- 1 teaspoon salt
- ½ teaspoon black pepper
- 1 bottle (12 ounces) Irish stout
- 1 cup beef broth
- 1 bay leaf
- 2 tablespoons finely chopped fresh parsley

1. Season ribs with salt and pepper. Heat oil in large skillet over medium-high heat until almost smoking. Cook ribs in batches, turning to brown all sides. Place ribs in slow cooker. Wipe out skillet with paper towel.

2. Cook bacon in same skillet over medium heat about 4 minutes or until crisp, stirring occasionally. Drain on paper towel-lined plate. Drain all but 1 tablespoon drippings from skillet.

3. Add onion to skillet; cook and stir until translucent. Add flour, mustard, tomato paste, 1 teaspoon salt and ½ teaspoon pepper; cook and stir 1 minute. Remove from heat; pour in stout, scraping up browned bits from bottom of skillet. Pour liquid over ribs in slow cooker. Add bacon, broth and bay leaf.

4. Cover; cook on LOW 8 hours or until ribs are fork-tender.

5. Skim fat from cooking liquid. Remove and discard bay leaf. Stir in parsley.

SAUERKRAUT PORK RIBS

MAKES 12 SERVINGS

1 tablespoon vegetable oil

3 to 4 pounds country-style pork ribs

1 large onion, thinly sliced

1 teaspoon caraway seeds

½ teaspoon garlic powder

¼ teaspoon black pepper

¾ cup water

1 jar (about 28 ounces) sauerkraut

6 medium red potatoes, quartered

1. Heat oil in large skillet over medium heat. Cook ribs in batches, turning to brown all sides. Place ribs in slow cooker. Drain excess fat from skillet.

2. Add onion to skillet; cook and stir until tender. Add caraway seeds, garlic powder and pepper; cook 15 minutes, stirring occasionally. Add onion mixture to slow cooker.

3. Add water to skillet, scraping up browned bits from bottom of skillet. Pour liquid into slow cooker. Partially drain sauerkraut, leaving some liquid; pour over ribs in slow cooker. Top with potatoes.

4. Cover; cook on LOW 6 to 8 hours or until potatoes are tender, stirring once during cooking.

RIO GRANDE RIBS

MAKES 6 SERVINGS

4 pounds country-style pork ribs, trimmed
    of all visible fat

    Salt, to taste

    Black pepper, to taste

1 jar (16 ounces) picante sauce

½ cup beer, nonalcoholic malt beverage or
    beef broth

¼ cup FRANK'S® REDHOT® Original Cayenne
    Pepper Sauce

1 teaspoon chili powder

2 cups FRENCH'S® French Fried Onions, divided

1. Season ribs with salt and pepper. Broil ribs
6 inches from heat on rack in broiler pan for
10 minutes or until well-browned, turning once.
Place ribs in slow cooker. Combine picante sauce,
beer, FRANK'S RedHot Sauce and chili powder in
small bowl. Pour mixture over ribs.

2. Cover and cook on LOW for 6 hours or on
HIGH for 3 hours or until ribs are tender. Transfer
ribs to serving platter; keep warm. Skim fat from
liquid.

3. Turn slow cooker to HIGH. Add *1 cup* French
Fried Onions to the liquid. Cook 10 to 15 minutes
or until slightly thickened. Spoon sauce over ribs
and sprinkle with remaining *1 cup* onions. Splash
on more FRANK'S RedHot Sauce to taste.

ON THE SIDE

MEXICAN-STYLE CORN ON THE COB

MAKES 4 SERVINGS

- 2 tablespoons mayonnaise
- ½ teaspoon chili powder
- ½ teaspoon grated lime peel
- 4 ears corn, shucked
- 2 tablespoons grated Parmesan cheese

1. Prepare grill for direct cooking.

2. Combine mayonnaise, chili powder and lime peel in small bowl; mix well.

3. Grill corn, uncovered, over medium-high heat 4 to 6 minutes or until lightly charred, turning several times. Immediately spread mayonnaise mixture over corn. Sprinkle with cheese.

GERMAN POTATO SALAD WITH GRILLED SAUSAGE

MAKES 6 TO 8 SERVINGS

⅔ cup prepared vinaigrette salad dressing

¼ cup FRENCH'S® Spicy Brown Mustard or FRENCH'S® Honey Dijon Mustard

1 tablespoon sugar

1½ pounds red or other boiling potatoes, cut into ¾-inch cubes

1 teaspoon salt

1 cup chopped green bell pepper

1 cup chopped celery

½ cup chopped onion

½ pound kielbasa or smoked sausage, split lengthwise

1. Combine salad dressing, mustard and sugar in large bowl; set aside.

2. Place potatoes in large saucepan. Add salt and enough water to cover potatoes. Heat to boiling. Cook 10 to 15 minutes until potatoes are tender. Drain and transfer to bowl with dressing. Add bell pepper, celery and onion. Set aside.

3. Grill sausage over medium-high heat until lightly browned and heated through. Cut into small cubes. Add to bowl with potatoes. Toss well to coat evenly. Serve warm.

JALAPEÑO CORN MUFFINS

MAKES 12 MUFFINS

Cooking spray

1 cup flour

1 cup yellow cornmeal

2 teaspoons baking powder

¼ teaspoon salt

2 eggs

½ cup KARO® Light Corn Syrup or KARO® Lite Syrup

¼ cup MAZOLA® Oil

1 cup cream-style corn

1 cup (4 ounces) shredded Monterey Jack cheese

2 tablespoons chopped seeded jalapeño peppers, fresh or pickled

1. Preheat oven to 400°F. Spray 12 (2½-inch) muffin pan cups with cooking spray.

2. In medium bowl combine flour, cornmeal, baking powder and salt.

3. In large bowl combine eggs, corn syrup and oil. Stir in flour mixture until well blended. Stir in corn, cheese and peppers. Spoon into prepared muffin pan cups.

4. Bake 15 to 20 minutes or until lightly browned and firm to touch. Cool in pan on wire rack 5 minutes; remove from pan.

PREP TIME: 15 minutes
BAKE TIME: 20 minutes, plus cooling

CLASSIC MACARONI AND CHEESE

MAKES 6 SERVINGS

3   tablespoons butter or margarine

¼   cup finely chopped onion (optional)

2   tablespoons all-purpose flour

½   teaspoon salt

⅛   teaspoon black pepper

2   cups milk

2   cups (8 ounces) SARGENTO® Fancy Shredded Mild Cheddar Cheese, divided

2   cups elbow macaroni, cooked and drained

Melt butter in medium saucepan over medium heat. Cook onion, if desired, in butter 5 minutes or until tender. Stir in flour, salt and pepper. Gradually add milk and cook, stirring occasionally, until thickened.

Remove from heat. Add 1½ cups cheese and stir until cheese is melted. Combine cheese sauce with cooked macaroni. Place in 1½-quart casserole; top with remaining cheese.

Bake in preheated 350°F oven 30 minutes or until bubbly and cheese is lightly browned.

PREP TIME: 15 minutes
COOK TIME: 30 minutes

SWEET POTATO FRIES

MAKES 2 TO 4 SERVINGS

1   teaspoon coarse salt

½   teaspoon black pepper

¼   teaspoon ground red pepper

2   large sweet potatoes, peeled

2   tablespoons vegetable oil

1. Preheat oven to 425°F. Line large baking sheet with foil; spray with nonstick cooking spray. Combine salt, black pepper and red pepper in small bowl; mix well.

2. Cut potatoes into long thin spears. Combine potatoes and oil in large bowl; toss to coat. Arrange potatoes in single layer on prepared baking sheet.

3. Bake 30 minutes or until lightly browned and crisp, turning once. Toss hot potatoes with seasoning mixture. Serve immediately.

CORN AND BLACK-EYED PEA SALAD

MAKES 8 SERVINGS

1   bag (16 ounces) frozen whole kernel corn, thawed (about 3 cups)

1   can (about 15 ounces) black-eyed peas, rinsed and drained

1   large green pepper, chopped (about 1 cup)

1   medium onion, chopped (about ½ cup)

½   cup chopped fresh cilantro leaves

1   jar (16 ounces) PACE® Picante Sauce

1. Stir the corn, peas, green pepper, onion and cilantro in a medium bowl. Add the picante sauce and stir to coat.

2. Cover and refrigerate for 4 hours. Stir before serving.

PREP TIME: 15 minutes
CHILL TIME: 4 hours
TOTAL TIME: 4 hours 15 minutes

KITCHEN TIP: Prepare the salad as directed. Cover and refrigerate overnight. Stir the salad before serving.

NEW ENGLAND BAKED BEANS

MAKES 4 TO 6 SERVINGS

- 4 slices bacon, chopped
- 3 cans (about 15 ounces each) Great Northern beans, rinsed and drained
- ¾ cup water
- 1 onion, chopped
- ⅓ cup canned diced tomatoes, well drained
- 3 tablespoons packed brown sugar
- 3 tablespoons maple syrup
- 3 tablespoons molasses
- 2 cloves garlic, minced
- ½ teaspoon salt
- ½ teaspoon dry mustard
- ⅛ teaspoon black pepper
- ½ bay leaf

Slow Cooker Directions

1. Cook bacon in large skillet over medium-high heat until almost chewy but not crisp. Drain on paper towel-lined plate. Combine bacon and remaining ingredients in slow cooker.

2. Cover; cook on LOW 6 to 8 hours or until thickened. Remove and discard bay leaf.

ROASTED POTATO SALAD WITH VEGETABLES

MAKES 4 TO 6 SERVINGS

- 4 to 5 small red potatoes, cut into 1-inch cubes (about 5 cups)
- 2 sweet potatoes, cut into 1-inch cubes (about 3 cups)
- ⅓ cup diced red onion
- 1 tablespoon plus 1 teaspoon olive oil
- 2 tablespoons COCA-COLA®
- 2 teaspoons balsamic vinegar
- 1 tablespoon packed brown sugar
  Salt and black pepper
- 2 cups green beans, cut into 1-inch pieces
- 2 large tomatoes, seeded and chopped
- 1 yellow, red or orange bell pepper, chopped

Dressing
- 3 tablespoons honey mustard
- 3 tablespoons COCA-COLA®
- 1 tablespoon mayonnaise
- 1 teaspoon balsamic vinegar

Preheat oven to 400°F. Mix red potatoes, sweet potatoes, onion, olive oil, 2 tablespoons *Coca-Cola*® and vinegar on rimmed baking sheet.

Sprinkle with brown sugar, salt and black pepper and mix to coat. Roast 17 to 20 minutes, until potatoes are browned and tender.

Meanwhile, steam green beans over boiling water until crisp-tender, about 3 to 4 minutes.

When potatoes and green beans are done, combine with tomatoes and bell peppers. Combine dressing ingredients. Add to vegetables and stir until all ingredients are coated. Serve hot or warm.

KOHLRABI AND CARROT SLAW

MAKES 8 SERVINGS

2   pounds kohlrabi bulbs, peeled and shredded

2   medium carrots, shredded

1   small red bell pepper, chopped

8   cherry tomatoes, halved

2   green onions, thinly sliced

¼   cup mayonnaise

¼   cup plain yogurt

2   tablespoons cider vinegar

2   tablespoons finely chopped fresh parsley

1   teaspoon dried dill weed

½   teaspoon salt

¼   teaspoon ground cumin

⅛   teaspoon black pepper

1. Combine kohlrabi, carrots, bell pepper, tomatoes and green onions in large bowl.

2. Combine mayonnaise, yogurt, vinegar, parsley, dill, salt, cumin and black pepper in medium bowl; mix well. Add to vegetables; toss to coat. Cover and refrigerate until ready to serve.

FIESTA CORN BREAD

MAKES 12 SERVINGS

- 2 cups all-purpose flour
- 1½ cups white or yellow cornmeal
- 1½ cups (6 ounces) shredded Cheddar cheese
- 1 can (7 ounces) ORTEGA® Fire-Roasted Diced Green Chiles
- ½ cup granulated sugar
- 1 tablespoon baking powder
- 1½ teaspoons salt
- 1 can (12 ounces) evaporated milk
- ½ cup vegetable oil
- 2 large eggs, lightly beaten

PREHEAT oven to 375°F. Grease 13×9-inch baking pan.

COMBINE flour, cornmeal, cheese, chiles, sugar, baking powder and salt in large bowl; mix well. Add evaporated milk, oil and eggs; stir just until moistened. Spread in prepared baking pan.

BAKE for 30 to 35 minutes or until wooden pick inserted in center comes out clean. Cool in pan on wire rack for 10 minutes; cut into squares. Serve warm.

PREP TIME: 10 minutes
START TO FINISH TIME: 45 minutes

SAVORY GREEN BEANS

MAKES 8 SERVINGS

8 cups frozen French-cut green beans, thawed and well drained

4 tablespoons (½ stick) butter, divided

2 cups coarsely chopped mushrooms

⅓ cup diced onion

⅓ cup diced celery

⅓ cup grated carrot

2 cups whipping cream

1 cup chicken broth

1 teaspoon salt

½ teaspoon black pepper

½ cup canned French fried onions

1. Preheat oven to 325°F. Place green beans in 2-quart casserole.

2. Melt 2 tablespoons butter in medium saucepan over medium heat. Add mushrooms; cook and stir 2 to 3 minutes or until softened. Remove to medium bowl.

3. Melt remaining 2 tablespoons butter in same saucepan. Add onion, celery and carrot; cook and stir 5 minutes or until onion is translucent. Stir in cream, broth, salt and pepper; bring to a boil. Reduce heat to low; simmer 12 to 15 minutes or until slightly thickened. Stir in mushrooms.

4. Pour mushroom mixture over green beans; mix well. Sprinkle with French fried onions.

5. Bake 25 minutes or until heated through.

UNCLE JOE'S BAKED BEANS

MAKES 4 SERVINGS

- 8 slices bacon, cut into ½-inch pieces
- 1 medium onion, chopped
- 1 can (12 ounces) COCA-COLA®
- 1 can (6 ounces) tomato paste
- 1 tablespoon Dijon mustard
- 1 teaspoon hot pepper sauce
- 2 cans (8 ounces each) crushed pineapple, drained
- 1 can (about 15 ounces) kidney beans, drained
- 1 can (about 15 ounces) pinto beans, drained

Cook bacon and onion in large skillet over medium-high heat until bacon is browned and crispy. Drain fat; set aside.

Preheat oven to 375°F. Spray 11×7-inch baking dish with nonstick cooking spray.

Combine *Coca-Cola*®, tomato paste, mustard and hot pepper sauce in large bowl; mix well. Add pineapple, beans and bacon mixture; mix well. Transfer to prepared baking dish. Bake, uncovered, 20 to 25 minutes or until beans are hot and bubbly.

TIP: Baked beans are a real crowd-pleaser! Serve this summer favorite alongside burgers at your next picnic, barbecue or family gathering.

CREAMY RED POTATO SALAD

MAKES 10 SERVINGS

- 3 pounds red bliss or new potatoes, cut into ¾-inch chunks
- ½ cup Italian vinaigrette dressing
- ¾ cup HELLMANN'S® or BEST FOODS® Real Mayonnaise
- ½ cup sliced green onions
- 1 teaspoon Dijon mustard
- 1 teaspoon lemon juice
- ⅛ teaspoon ground black pepper

1. Cover potatoes with water in 4-quart saucepot; bring to a boil over medium-high heat. Reduce heat to low and simmer 10 minutes or until potatoes are tender. Drain and cool slightly.

2. Combine all ingredients except potatoes in large salad bowl. Add potatoes and toss gently. Serve chilled or at room temperature.

PREP TIME: 15 minutes
COOK TIME: 10 minutes

COUNTRY-STYLE CORN

MAKES 6 TO 8 SERVINGS

4   slices bacon

1   tablespoon all-purpose flour

1   can (about 15 ounces) corn, drained

1   can (about 15 ounces) cream-style corn

1   red bell pepper, diced

½   cup sliced green onions
    Salt and black pepper

1. Cook bacon in large skillet over medium heat until crisp; drain on paper towel-lined plate. Crumble bacon; set aside.

2. Whisk flour into drippings in skillet. Add corn, cream-style corn and bell pepper; bring to a boil. Reduce heat to low; cook 10 minutes or until thickened, stirring occasionally.

3. Stir in green onions and bacon. Season with salt and black pepper.

SWEET AND SAVORY SWEET POTATO SALAD

MAKES 6 SERVINGS

- 4 cups chopped cooked peeled sweet potatoes (about 4 to 6)
- ¾ cup chopped green onions
- ½ cup chopped fresh parsley
- ½ cup dried unsweetened cherries
- ¼ cup plus 2 tablespoons rice wine vinegar
- 2 tablespoons extra virgin olive oil
- 2 tablespoons coarse ground mustard
- ¾ teaspoon salt
- ¾ teaspoon garlic powder
- ¼ teaspoon black pepper

1. Combine sweet potatoes, green onions, parsley and cherries in large bowl.

2. Whisk vinegar, oil, mustard, salt, garlic powder and pepper in small bowl until well blended. Pour over sweet potato mixture; toss gently to coat. Serve immediately or cover and refrigerate until ready to serve.

SPICY CITRUS SLAW

MAKES 4 CUPS

- 1 cup HELLMANN'S® or BEST FOODS® Canola Cholesterol Free Mayonnaise
- 1 can (11 ounces) mandarin oranges, drained (reserve 2 tablespoons syrup)
- 2 teaspoons apple cider vinegar
- 1 tablespoon chopped fresh cilantro (optional)

  Hot pepper sauce to taste
- ½ teaspoon salt
- 1 bag (16 ounces) coleslaw mix

In large bowl, combine Hellmann's® or Best Foods® Canola Cholesterol Free Mayonnaise, reserved syrup, vinegar, cilantro, hot pepper sauce and salt. Stir in coleslaw mix and oranges. Chill, if desired.

PREP TIME: 15 Minutes

INDEX

ACKNOWLEDGMENTS

The publisher would like to thank the companies and organizations listed below for the use of their recipes and photographs in this publication.

ACH Food Companies, Inc.

Campbell Soup Company

Grandma's®, A Division of B&G Foods North America, Inc.

Ortega®, A Division of B&G Foods North America, Inc.

Reckitt Benckiser LLC.

Recipes courtesy of the Reynolds Kitchens

Sargento® Foods Inc.

Unilever

METRIC CONVERSION CHART

VOLUME MEASUREMENTS (dry)

1/8 teaspoon = 0.5 mL
1/4 teaspoon = 1 mL
1/2 teaspoon = 2 mL
3/4 teaspoon = 4 mL
1 teaspoon ≐ 5 mL
1 tablespoon = 15 mL
2 tablespoons = 30 mL
1/4 cup = 60 mL
1/3 cup = 75 mL
1/2 cup = 125 mL
2/3 cup = 150 mL
3/4 cup = 175 mL
1 cup = 250 mL
2 cups = 1 pint = 500 mL
3 cups = 750 mL
4 cups = 1 quart = 1 L

VOLUME MEASUREMENTS (fluid)

1 fluid ounce (2 tablespoons) = 30 mL
4 fluid ounces (1/2 cup) = 125 mL
8 fluid ounces (1 cup) = 250 mL
12 fluid ounces (1 1/2 cups) = 375 mL
16 fluid ounces (2 cups) = 500 mL

WEIGHTS (mass)

1/2 ounce = 15 g
1 ounce = 30 g
3 ounces = 90 g
4 ounces = 120 g
8 ounces = 225 g
10 ounces = 285 g
12 ounces = 360 g
16 ounces = 1 pound = 450 g

DIMENSIONS

1/16 inch = 2 mm
1/8 inch = 3 mm
1/4 inch = 6 mm
1/2 inch = 1.5 cm
3/4 inch = 2 cm
1 inch = 2.5 cm

OVEN TEMPERATURES

250°F = 120°C
275°F = 140°C
300°F = 150°C
325°F = 160°C
350°F = 180°C
375°F = 190°C
400°F = 200°C
425°F = 220°C
450°F = 230°C

BAKING PAN SIZES

Utensil	Size in Inches/Quarts	Metric Volume	Size in Centimeters
Baking or Cake Pan (square or rectangular)	8×8×2	2 L	20×20×5
	9×9×2	2.5 L	23×23×5
	12×8×2	3 L	30×20×5
	13×9×2	3.5 L	33×23×5
Loaf Pan	8×4×3	1.5 L	20×10×7
	9×5×3	2 L	23×13×7
Round Layer Cake Pan	8×1½	1.2 L	20×4
	9×1½	1.5 L	23×4
Pie Plate	8×1¼	750 mL	20×3
	9×1¼	1 L	23×3
Baking Dish or Casserole	1 quart	1 L	—
	1½ quart	1.5 L	—
	2 quart	2 L	—